THE LITTLE BOOK OF
KIWIANA

Published in 2023 by OH!
An Imprint of Welbeck Non-Fiction Limited,
part of Welbeck Publishing Group.
Based in London and Sydney.
www.welbeckpublishing.com

Compilation text © Welbeck Non-Fiction Limited 2022
Design © Welbeck Non-Fiction Limited 2022

Disclaimer:

ISBN 978-1-80069-340-1

Compiled and written by: Pete Carter
Editorial: Victoria Denne
Project manager: Russell Porter
Design: Tony Seddon
Production: Jess Brisley

A CIP catalogue record for this book is available from the British Library

Printed in China

10 9 8 7 6 5 4 3 2 1

Cover image: Joanne Lush/Shutterstock. Other images: Freepix

THE LITTLE BOOK OF
KIWIANA

CONTENTS

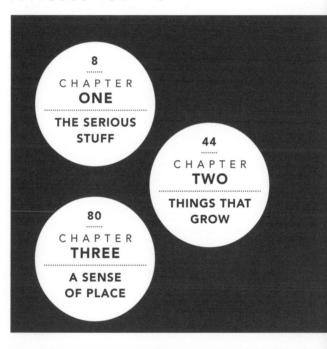

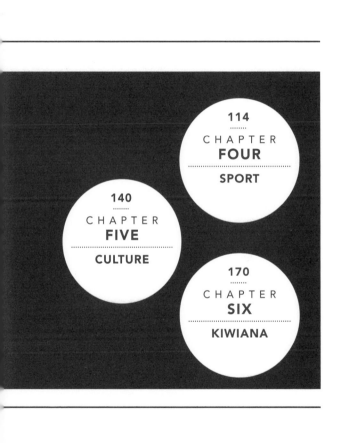

INTRODUCTION

Polynesians were the first people to settle in New Zealand about 1,000 years ago and became the indigenous Māori. This little book deliberately does not cover Māori history, culture and mythology, only because its importance is too great to cover in such a small volume.

Because of their isolation, the Islands were pretty much the last land masses on the planet to be inhabited. It's a country of extremes, about 10% bigger than the UK, with approximately 60 million fewer people living there. In the north the climate is sub-tropical, whereas the islands to the south are called Subantarctic for a reason. The mountains reach heights five times that of those in the UK. There are volcanoes, earthquakes and extreme weather. In the past 100 years the country has warmed by 1°C.

Abel Tasman was the first European to pass by, followed by Captain James Cook. Whalers, sealers and gold miners followed. In the meantime the Māori were trading with the convict settlements over the ditch in Sydney. Some intrepid locals headed north, and the first recorded visit was Moehanga of Ngāpuhi in 1806. Some New Zealanders celebrate 27 April as the day he discovered the United Kingdom, a nice twist on the usual story.

Since the cultures merged, much has gone right and much has gone wrong. Undoubtedly the country was colonised and the repairs necessary are still being undertaken. At the same time the country has been growing and maturing, enjoying and ruing its geographic isolation.

What are the first thoughts of non-New Zealanders when they think of the country? For many it will be the All Blacks, for others Kiri Te Kanawa; for some it will be yachting, for others Sir Edmund Hillary – whatever floats your boat I suppose.

CHAPTER
ONE

THE SERIOUS STUFF

To understand a country you have to have a sense of the history of the place. Human history in New Zealand is comparatively short and, like they say in some obituaries, the country has just packed so much in.

So here is a potted obituary of New Zealand – that's why it's serious.

About 85 million years ago New Zealand broke away from the supercontinent Gondwanaland.

Since then the country has been out on its own in geological terms and consequently developed its very own distinct flora and fauna.

Before people arrived, birds virtually had the country to themselves. Captain Cook, on arriving there, described the dawn chorus as "deafening".

The majority of birds were unique to New Zealand, whereas the only indigenous mammals were a native bat and seals that spend most of their time in the sea.

"

Despite a plethora of amateur
theories about Melanesian,
South American, Egyptian,
Phoenician and Celtic colonisation
of New Zealand, there is not a shred
of evidence that the first human
settlers were anything other than
Polynesian.

"

Michael King, *The Penguin History of New Zealand*, 2004

The Polynesian settlers brought kūmara (sweet potato), taro, yam and gourds with them and were proficient gardeners.

Great care would have to have been taken to ensure the precious plants survived the journey.

They also successfully brought over dogs and rats, but there is speculation that pigs and chickens did not survive the initial voyages.

The current consensus is
that the first settlers arrived from
somewhere in Polynesia about
800 years ago, during a period of
cultural expansion.

Navigating by stars, currents
and the prevailing winds,
Polynesians were the most widely
dispersed people on the planet
at the time according to historian
Michael King.

Obsidian flakes from the Bay of Plenty area used as tools have been found on the Kermadec Islands, suggesting that the voyages from Polynesia to New Zealand were return trips.

Birds had the run of
the country before settlers
arrived and suffered badly not just
from humans arriving but
from the animals they brought
with them.

Many native birds ground-nested
– especially understandable when
you can't fly – and, initially, had
no fear of man.

The early Māori were great gardeners and planted the crops they brought with them. Of course the climate was different from where they had arrived, especially the further south they travelled.

The warmer climate together with the greater fertility of the volcanic soils meant a larger density of population in the North Island.

The Dutchman Abel
Tasman was the first
known European to see the
country, in 1642. Four of
his men were killed
in a skirmish off
Golden Bay when
they tried to land
and restock
their water.

Golden Bay

Captain Cook liked New Zealand so much he went three times.

He is of course responsible for a lot of the early names of the country. For example, Young Nicks Head, named after the lad on the ship who first spotted land from the *Endeavour* on his first trip, and Aoraki/Mount Cook, the highest mountain.

Cook also introduced
the first pigs, as a
potential food source for
those who were to follow,
and the antecedents are
still here – gloriously
named
Captain Cookers.

HMS *Endeavour* was
a second-hand converted
coal carrier, a collier.
Cook learned his trade on
this type of ship.

He is acknowledged as an
extraordinary navigator
and map maker. The
epitome of a working-class
boy made good.

During the late 18th century and beginning of the 19th century there was extensive trade between Māori and the early settlement of Sydney.

According to the *Dictionary of Sydney,* many traders and sailors spoke Māori to facilitate transactions. Some attribute the success of Sydney to this trading relationship.

In the early 19th century, muskets, introduced as a result of trade, changed the way inter-tribal wars were fought.

Some estimates have it that up to 20,000 Māori were killed in the "Musket Wars" of this period.

Te Tiriti o Waitangi –
The Treaty of Waitangi,
New Zealand's foundational
constitutional document, was
signed on 6 February 1840 by
representatives of Queen Victoria
and various Māori chiefs.

It was drafted in English and
translated into Māori – which
partly explains why it is still a
controversial document.

The treaty is named after the place in the Bay of Islands where it was first signed. It was also signed in other places in 1840.

It wasn't until 1934 that the treaty was formally celebrated for the first time.

February the 6th is now marked as the public holiday "Waitangi Day".

New Zealand became an official colony of Britain in 1841.

In 1907 it became a Dominion.

Between the 1840s and early 1870s the New Zealand Wars took place. These were effectively between Colonial forces on one side and the Māori on the other.

The fighting was caused by land disputes, and 18,000 British troops were involved at its peak.

Chinese miners were invited into New Zealand in the 1860s to work the gold mines.

In 1881 a Poll Tax was specifically applied to Chinese migrants.

The government officially apologized for this in 2002.

New Zealand was the first country to allow women to vote in a national election, in 1893, though it was some 26 years later before they were allowed to stand for Parliament themselves.

First Woman MP:
Elizabeth McCombs (1933)

First Māori Woman MP:
Iriaka Rātana (1949)

ANZAC Day on 25 April commemorates the Gallipoli campaign, when New Zealand and Australian troops landed on the Turkish Peninsula in 1915 to secure the Dardanelles.

Winston Churchill planned the campaign. It failed miserably.

An estimated 130,000 men died, including 2,779 New Zealanders. It is seen as a foundational moment in New Zealand history as well as in Australia and Turkey.

ANZAC Day became a full public holiday in 1921, having been first commemorated in 1916.

The tiny settlement of Tinui in the Wairarapa claims to have had the first formal celebration.

Up to 2,000 visitors now visit on ANZAC Day – Tinui has a population of 25.

German raider ships laid mines in New Zealand waters in both world wars.

In the Second World War these raiders sunk several New Zealand and Allied merchant ships.

In both world wars German and Austrian citizens were interned, specifically on Matiu/Somes Island in Wellington Harbour and Motuihe Island in the Hauraki Gulf.

Count Felix von Luckner escaped from the latter in 1917 before being recaptured.

800 Japanese prisoners of war were held in Featherston in the Wairarapa.

In February 1943, a riot broke out resulting in the deaths of 48 prisoners and one guard.

The UK joined the EU in 1973 and basically abandoned New Zealand.

At that stage approximately half of the country's exports went straight to Britain.

Now about 2.5% of exports go there and China takes more than ten times that.

In 1985 the French Secret Service bombed and sank the Greenpeace ship *Rainbow Warrior* in Auckland Harbour, killing the Portugal-born photographer Fernando Pereira.

This followed the government under David Lange banning nuclear-powered or armed ships from entering New Zealand waters in 1984.

"

We are an enemy of the nuclear threat and we are an enemy of testing nuclear weapons in the South Pacific. New Zealand did not buy into this fight. France put agents into New Zealand. France put spies into New Zealand. France lets off bombs in the Pacific. France puts its President in the Pacific to crow about it.

"

David Lange, former Prime Minister of New Zealand

Only two
US Presidents have
visited New Zealand:

Lyndon B. Johnson,
in 1966, and
Bill Clinton, in 1999.

There have been three female Prime Ministers of New Zealand.

Jenny Shipley (National) served from 1997–1999 and Helen Clark (Labour), who became the first one to be elected, served from 1999–2008.

The current Prime Minister, Jacinda Ardern (Labour), was first elected in 2017 and, as of 2022, is mid-way through her second term.

In 2004 the Supreme Court was opened for business. Up until then the final right of appeal was to the Judicial Committee of the Privy Council in London.

On 15 March 2019 –
described by Jacinda
Ardern as "one of New
Zealand's darkest days",
a white supremacist
murdered 51 people
at two Christchurch
mosques.

"

They will remain with
us forever.

They are us.

But with that memory
comes a responsibility.

A responsibility to be the
place that we wish to be.

A place that is diverse, that
is welcoming, that is kind
and compassionate.

Those values represent
the very best of us.

But even the ugliest of
viruses can exist in places
they are not welcome.

Racism exists, but it is
not welcome here.

Jacinda Ardern, 29 March 2019

CHAPTER
TWO

THINGS THAT GROW

(SOME OF WHICH ARE EATEN)

It's well documented that when the first people arrived in New Zealand, there were no land mammals, so everything they were able to eat either grew here, swam here or had feathers.

Since then, many edible creatures have been introduced and they now contribute to nearly 70% of the country's total exported goods.

Moas were large, flightless birds that thrived on the land, growing up to 3.6 metres (12 feet) tall and weighing up to 230 kg.

They were an excellent source of protein for the early settlers and their eggs were used as water carriers.

New Zealand has no native
mammals other than
two species of bats and sea
mammals.

It does have the Tuatara, a
lizard that looks like a
dinosaur. Living for up to
100 years, it can grow to 50 cm
(1.6 ft) and weigh 1.5 kg. It is
currently under threat.

The greater spotted kiwi is the largest of the species, and like all kiwi cannot fly.

Females are larger than the male, reaching up to 50 cm tall and 3.3 kg in weight.

In 2021 the New Zealand Bird of the Year competition was won by a bat. The long-tailed bat, also known as pekapeka-tou-roa, which is no bigger than a thumb, got the most votes.

The klākāpō was Bird of the Year in 2020.

In 2022 a female godwit made the longest flight ever recorded by a land bird.

She travelled non-stop from Alaska to New Zealand, a journey of 12,200 km that took eight days and 12 hours at an average speed of 59 km/h. A godwit weighs 290 grams.

66

That is one of the funniest things I've ever seen. You are being shagged by a rare parrot.

99

Stephen Fry on Codfish Island filming the flightless kākāpō with zoologist Mark Carwadine for the BBC

Sheep numbers in New Zealand have decreased from 70 million in 1982 – "Peak Sheep" – to 26 million in 2022. Or, in other words, down from 22 sheep per person to only 5.

Captain Cook – of course – introduced the first breeding pair, which died days later having eaten the wrong sort of food.

The advent of refrigerated shipping changed New Zealand agriculture for ever.

The first cargo of frozen lamb was sent to London in 1882.

There are approximately two cows for each person in New Zealand – one dairy and one beef. This is about 14 times as many as the global average.

Possums were first introduced in 1837 for the fur trade, but they didn't survive. Twenty years later, another cohort were released, and this lot definitely took hold.

Due to conservation efforts, their number is down to an estimated 30 million, from 70 million in the 1980s.

In Australia, possums are coveted and protected, whereas they are unwanted in New Zealand.

Introduced Pests and Predators

Possums

Deer

Goats

Stoats, weasels, ferrets

Feral cats

Tahr

Pigs

Rabbits

Rats

Mice

Wallabies

Frogs

New Zealand aims to be predator-free by 2050.

66

While once the greatest threat to our native wildlife was poaching and deforestation, it is now introduced predators.

99

John Key, Prime Minister 2008–2016

Moose were released in Fiordland in 1910, but the last physical evidence of them was found in the 1930s. The last photograph of a moose was taken in the 1950s, but they are still "seen". The last sighting was reported in 2020.

Pōhutukawa

Known as the New Zealand Christmas Tree, the Pōhutukawa's reddy crimson blossoms appear over the festive period. It can grow as high as 25 metres (82 ft).

An attractive tree, it has been exported. Its roots have been blamed for sewer damage in San Francisco and it is listed as an invasive species in South Africa.

Cordyline australis

Another exported tree found around the world, *Cordyline australis* is especially prevalent in the UK, where it is known as the Torquay Palm. It is not actually a palm. At home it is known as tī kōuka, or Cabbage Tree.

To the Māori the tree was a great source of fibre for ropes and clothing as well as a source of food.

Kūmara

Brought to New Zealand by the first inhabitants from Polynesia, this sweet potato was grown in gardens and stored over winter as the climate was too cold to grow the vegetable.

It is still a staple across the country enjoyed for its vitamins and fibre.

Kiwifruit

The Chinese gooseberry appears to have arrived almost by accident in the early 20th century. The name was changed as a marketing ploy in the 1950s.

It is still New Zealand's highest-earning horticultural export, though the largest-producing nation of kiwifruit is now China.

Whitebait

A delicacy within New Zealand, during the season whitebaiters jealously guard their patch of river to scoop these baby fish out.

There are five native fish that make up the fishery and four out of these are now on the endangered list. Eating the babies is clearly not the best way to preserve a species.

Usually they are served up as an omelette and the entire fish is eaten.

Bluff Oysters

Famous in New Zealand, Bluff oysters are pulled out of the sea in the Foveaux Strait between the bottom of the South Island and Stewart Island.

At the beginning of the season helicopters meet the boats to ensure their oysters are first to table in Auckland and Wellington restaurants.

Pavlova

A contentious food only in the sense that Australia wrongly claim this meringue and cream dessert as their own, Pavlova is named after the Russian ballerina who rather annoyingly visited both countries and never proclaimed who invented the pudding first. She toured New Zealand in 1926 and died five years later, aged 49.

Jaffas

Another national icon, Jaffas
are chocolate balls coated in an
orange-flavoured confectionary.
An annual race is held down the
steepest street in the world in
Dunedin, where 30,000 are let go
and raced from top to bottom.

Pineapple Lumps

These were originally invented as a means of using up waste from other lollies.

Incidentally, New Zealanders, like their Australian cousins, call their confectionary "lollies".

The English would call them "sweets"; the Americans "candy".

In 2020 approximately 350 million litres of wine was produced, seven times more than was produced in 1990.

Sauvignon blanc makes up at least two thirds of this. The wine industry exported NZ$2bn worth in the same year.

According to the New Zealand Winegrowers association, Samuel Marsden, an Anglican missionary, made the first recorded planting of grapevines, at the Bay of Islands in 1819.

The earliest recorded winemaker was Scotsman James Busby, appointed the first British Resident in New Zealand. When the French explorer Dumont d'Urville visited Busby at Waitangi in 1840, he was given "a light white wine, very sparkling and delicious to taste..."

In 2022, over NZ$400m worth of honey will be exported from New Zealand. Most of this will be high-value mānuka honey, prized for its antibacterial properties.

It is legal in New Zealand
to distil your own liquor,
which leaves the country
as an outlier among
Western nations and
could partly explain the
explosion of distilling
companies set up locally
in recent times.

Lemon and Paeroa is a local hero soft drink, invented in 1907 to combine lemon juice with carbonated mineral water extracted from the springs at the town of Paeroa.

It is now produced by Coca-Cola in a factory in Auckland.

Who brewed the first
beer in New Zealand?

Why, Captain Cook of
course, to prevent his crew
contracting scurvy.

Flat White

Some say the Flat White originated in Wellington in 1989 when a despondent barista named Fraser McInnes made a cappuccino with low-fat milk that refused to froth.

With typical Kiwi positivity, he named the failed cappuccino Flat White, and the term stuck.

Australia also lays claim to an earlier invention.

Meat pies

A phenomenon that didn't originate in New Zealand, but something of which New Zealanders are particularly proud, are meat pies. The annual 'Bakels New Zealand Supreme Pie Award' is keenly competed for.

Caught on a popular TV show, a NZ Police officer once famously gave a stopped suspect the advice: "Always blow on the pie."

Anchor Butter

A brand since 1886, when allegedly the name was chosen by the formerly Cornish immigrant dairy farmer, having seen an anchor tattoo on an employee's arm, Anchor butter is now owned by Kiwi dairy behemoth Fonterra.

Those that grew up in the UK eating the product will be disappointed that the butter there is now produced locally.

Southland Sushi

Known in the rest of the world
as a cheese roll.

Ladies, a plate

If you are invited for morning or afternoon tea, it will often be with this somewhat sexist instruction, meaning "please bring some home cooking to share with the other assembled guests".

There are stories of recent arrivals into the country attending gatherings with an empty plate, assuming the hosts didn't have enough crockery.

Kiwi Onion Dip

Made with a can of reduced cream and a packet of dehydrated onion soup, mixed together and chilled and served with corn chips while the meat is overcooked on the barbecue.

CHAPTER
THREE

A SENSE OF PLACE

Giving some idea of the
scale, geographic and geological
variety of the country from
top to bottom.

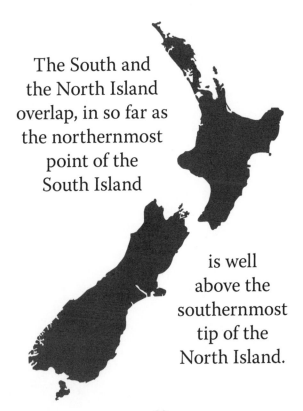

The South and
the North Island
overlap, in so far as
the northernmost
point of the
South Island

is well
above the
southernmost
tip of the
North Island.

"

New Zealand, the world's
biggest film set, is also the
world's must-visit destination
for the umpteenth year in a row –
no wonder the locals are smiling.
They've long known they live in
paradise, and now everyone
else does too.

"

Lonely Planet Guide

Cape Reinga

Cape Reinga is generally thought of as the most northerly point of New Zealand. In fact, North Cape, as perhaps you'd expect it to be, is further north.

The Bluff

Likewise, the Bluff is supposed to be the southern-most point, but it's not. Slope Point in the Catlins is further south.

"

We landed at Auckland,
and there were cows either
side of the runway. It was
a bit of a shock – I thought
we'd landed on a farm.
I was twelve.

"

Muhammad, a new New Zealander, interviewee in
This Is Us – New Zealanders in our own words

New Zealand loves its giant motifs

There is a huge carrot in Ohakune, and an oversize bottle of Lemon and Paeroa in the eponymous town. There's also massive fruit in Cromwell, a salmon in Rakaia, a crayfish in Kaikōura.

But the piece de resistance is surely the giant gumboot in Taihape. The town is the self-proclaimed gumboot capital of the world and hosts the national gumboot-throwing competition.

If Wellington was in the Northern Hemisphere its latitude would be closest to Barcelona in Spain.

It is the most southerly capital city.

There are 13
National Parks in New
Zealand and three
designated UNESCO
World Heritage Areas;
these are Tongariro
National Park,
Te Wāhipounamu, and
the Subantarctic Islands.

Aotearoa is generally accepted as the Māori word for New Zealand, the rough translation being, "Land of the Long White Cloud".

"The Shaky Isles" is a well known and appropriate nickname for the country, especially by Australians. There are approximately 14,000 earthquakes a year, but only 150 or so are felt. In 2011, a 6.3 hit Christchurch and caused 181 deaths.

Australia

Sometimes known in New Zealand as "The West Island".

New Zealanders often refer to their country as Godzone, as in "God's own country".
In early 2022, a new joke was doing the rounds:

"

A guy I know bumped into God
at a café in Wellington the other day.
He asked her,
'What are you doing here, mate?'

God said,
'Working from home, bro.'

"

Facebook joke – unattributed

Weather extremes

Hottest recorded temperature
42.4°C (108°F), Rangiora,
South Island, 1973

Coldest recorded temperature
-25.6°C (-14°F), Ranfurly,
South Island, 1903

The **wettest** place in NZ
recorded over 16 metres of rain
in a calendar year;
the lowest was 212 mm in a year.

Aoraki/Mt Cook is the
highest peak in
Australasia at 3,724 metres
(12,218 feet).

The first ascent was
in 1894.

The Whanganui River, the third longest in New Zealand, was given legal personhood in 2017.

The Te Aroroa Trail is a 3,000 km continuous walk from Cape Reinga to the Bluff, officially opened in 2011.

Walkers completing the whole trail take between three and six months.

Wikipedia lists ten candidates for the 8th wonder of the natural world. One of them was the Pink and White terraces near Rotorua that the early Victorian travellers lined up to visit even though it would take a six-month round trip.

Unfortunately, a volcanic eruption in 1886 wiped these out. Luckily for New Zealand, it has another one on the list – Milford Sound – and a celebrity endorser – Rudyard Kipling, who visited in 1891.

Rotorua is famous for its geothermal activity, much of which is used to generate electricity.

The Pōhutu Geyser is now the largest in the Southern Hemisphere and can reach 30 metres (100 ft).

The Waimangu Geyser used to be the biggest in the world and would reach a height of 450 metres (1,476 ft), but it stopped blowing in 1904.

Taumata
whakat
angihan
gakoaua
uotamat
eaturip
ukakapik
imaunga
horonuk
upokaiw
henuaki
tanatahu

This is the longest place name in the world, at 85 letters long.

It roughly translates as: "the summit where Tamatea, the man with the big knees, the slider, climber of mountains, the land-swallower who travelled about, played his nose flute to his loved one."

In 1908 *Spectator* magazine declared that Milford Track was "the finest walk in the world".

It is now one of ten designated Great Walks of New Zealand – on one of these you don't even walk; you paddle for four days down the Whanganui River.

Auckland/*Tāmaki Makaurau*
is New Zealand's largest city
and in 2022 had 1.65 million
inhabitants. It is very much the
nation's commercial centre.
It is built on a volcanic
field of 53 volcanoes.

Aukland

The most recent
eruption was on
Rangitoto Island, 600
years ago, so it would
have had human
witnesses.

Wellington/*Te Whanganui-a-Tara*/*Pōneke* has been New Zealand's capital since 1865 and is home to the New Zealand Parliament, including the infamous Beehive building that houses the Executive wing of the government. The population of the metro area in 2022 was 419,000 (this includes the cities of Lower Hutt, Upper Hutt and Porirua).

Wellington

66

We've lived all over the world, and Wellington is hard to beat – not just on a good day.

99

Antony, interviewee,
This Is Us – New Zealanders in our own words

New Zealand has had three capitals. The first was Okiato in the Bay of Islands in 1840, then Auckland in 1841 and Wellington in 1865. The latter move was a salve to the South Island, which was expanding rapidly at the time.

Christchurch/*Ōtautahi* is the largest city in the South Island and has a population of 402,000. Known as the Garden City, it is still regarded as the most "English" of New Zealand's towns and cities.

Christchurch

Dunedin/*Ōtepoti*, with a population of 114,000, has been overtaken by other cities in terms of population but has historically been regarded as the fourth city. During the Goldrush of the 1860s it was for a short while the largest centre, and certainly a lot of the city's wealth goes back to that time. New Zealand's oldest university, Otago, is situated there.

Dunedin

There are eight universities in the country:

Otago, Auckland, Victoria, Canterbury, Waikato, Massey, Lincoln and AUT (Auckland University of Technology).

Auckland is commonly accepted as the highest ranked university in New Zealand.

66

Auckland is all about how much money you have, Wellington is about the job you have, Christchurch is about which school you went to, and Dunedin – well who really gives a stuff.

99

Jac, artist

Queenstown

Queenstown basks in its reputation as the Adventure Capital of New Zealand, while some claim it is more than that and is the adventure capital of the world.

Whatever it is, you can throw yourself out of planes, off mountains and bridges; you can ski, snowboard, jetboat and luge. Most of these, of course, will cost you money.

"

Because New Zealand is dwarfed by Australia, people think we're teeny-tiny, but actually it's just that Australia is so enormous. The North Island alone is a fourteen-hour drive top to bottom and the South Island is another eleven hours. We do however only have five million people.

"

Sue Fitzmaurice, writer

Rough Guides readers have voted New Zealand the most beautiful country in the world in 2022.

According to the same publication it was only third in 2017, behind Canada and Scotland.

CHAPTER
FOUR

SPORT

New Zealanders love their sport.

While the All Blacks may be
the most recognized team globally,
New Zealands sports men and
women have run, swam, rowed and
competed at international level, and
have world champions and record
holders across many disciplines.

It's difficult not to say that they
punch above their weight.

Over half of
New Zealand's 137
Olympic medals were
won in sitting-down
sports: rowing, canoeing,
sailing, equestrian
and cycling.

"

Laugh or cry, it's your choice, isn't it? I don't feel anger but there's a lot of disappointment. This game is fickle at times.

"

Kane Williams, New Zealand Cricket Captain,
after losing the 2019 Cricket One-Day World Cup Final
to England in a super over

66

Let me repeat that: Valerie Adams won every major international meet she competed in from the 2006 Commonwealth Games to the 2014 Commonwealth Games.

That's nine whole years of winning everything: 3 x Commonwealth Games, 4 x World Outdoor Championships, 4 x World Indoor Championships, and 2 x Olympics. Adams' winning streak for internationally ranked meets was 56. That's just so many competitions.

99

Madeleine Chapman in the *Spinoff*

"

New Zealand, we have this …
culture of tall poppy syndrome,
… When you see one of us rising,
you want to tear him down,
because you feel inadequate and
you want to call it humble. I am
extraordinarily humble, believe me,
but you'll never know that, because
you'll never get to know me.

"

Israel Adesanya, Mixed Martial Arts Champion, in his
Sportsman of the Year 2019 award speech

Arthur Lydiard – athletics coach 1917–2004

Arthur coached many New Zealand athletes including three-time Olympic Gold medallist Peter Snell.

While coaching his Olympians, Lydiard worked as a milkman and hand-made his athletes' running shoes.

“

What I love about my sport is
that I get to be strong. I can help
my boyfriend lift fridges into
the house, or new equipment,
couches…

It's cool to have that strength to
be able to help around.

”

Lisa Carrington, five-time Olympic Gold medallist kayaker

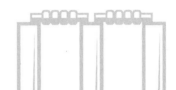

One that got away

New Zealand-born cricketer Ben Stokes, 2022 England Captain.

Over 40 years later, New Zealand is still not over the underarm incident.

In 1981, Australian cricket captain Greg Chappell ordered his younger brother Trevor to bowl underarm to the batsman Brian McKechnie, therefore ensuring the home team won in Melbourne.

In 1967, Denny Hulme became the only New Zealander thus far to win a Formula One World Championship.

Scott Dixon is still racing and has won the Indy Car Championship six times.

Competitive
sheep shearing

"

Shearing as a sport demands not only mental toughness and physical strength, but dexterity and finesse. Tactics play a role, but sheep provide a chance element. Judges are there to ensure corners, the animal or the wool are not cut. Once you see competitive shearing, you are struck by its physicality and a rhythmic grace.

"

Jeanette Maxwell in the *Southland Times*

Anthony Wilding is the only New Zealand tennis player to win a major title.

He won 11 Grand Slam events including 4 titles at Wimbledon, the last in 1913.

He was killed in action in France in 1915, aged 31. He was regarded as the first "superstar" of tennis.

Sir David Alexander Fagan, KNZM, born in 1961, is a New Zealand sheep shearer living on Te Kuiti cattle farm, who has won the New Zealand Golden Shears contest a record 16 times.

Setting 10 world records and winning 5 world, 6 world team and 16 national titles makes him New Zealand's most successful competition sheep shearer, and he continues to win nationally and internationally.

Yachting

Since Alan Bond shocked the yachting world in 1983 by winning the Americas Cup from the Americans for Australia, New Zealand has won the trophy four times out of the twelve times it has been held.

New Zealand will defend their next title in the not so well known New Zealand city of Barcelona in 2024. Money talks.

In 1884, Cantabrian William Atack was the first person to use a whistle as a referee. Up until then they had had to use their voices.

Sports team naming

The All Blacks were first and need no introduction, but they started a whole class of New Zealand-specific national sports team naming. Any colour you like, as long as it is black, white or silver.

Black Ferns – Women's rugby

All Whites – Men's football

Black Caps – Men's cricket

Black Jacks – Lawn bowls

Silver Ferns – Women's netball

Tall Blacks – Men's basketball

Wheel Blacks – Wheelchair rugby

Badminton in New Zealand did try **Black Cocks** for a while, but as the *New Zealand Herald* reported in 2005, the national body went "soft" on endorsing the name.

Phar Lap is regarded as
New Zealand's most famous horse,
but never raced there.

He foaled near Timaru in 1926,
was trained in Australia (where he
is also regarded as an Australian
great) and then died in controversial
circumstances in California in 1932.

His oversized heart is in a bottle in
Canberra, while his skeleton is kept at
Te Papa Museum in Wellington.

All Blacks win record

At time of writing:
played 612,
won 472, drawn 22
and lost 118.

A win record of 77%.

All Black records

Most tests – Richie McCaw, 148

Most points – Dan Carter, 1,598

Most tries – Doug Howlett, 49

As of May 2022, 1,199 players
have played for the All Blacks

"

The Kurow pub is like a church, but here they worship rugby, beer... and this guy.

"

Reporter Hadyn Jones, on Richie McCaw

The first All Blacks to tour
outside New Zealand left for
Europe in 1905. They played 35
games and only lost one to Wales
3-0, setting the tone for future
success very early.

The 1981 Springbok Tour was a defining moment in New Zealand. It divided the country into those who thought that sport and politics were not connected and those who did, especially the view that playing South Africa condoned apartheid.

It was not a happy time and the divisions took a long time to heal. The tour went ahead although two games were cancelled.

"

I feel that if I am busting my arse, if I am stretching at night, if I am working hard in the gym, if I am doing all of my extras out on the field, if I am the first one there and the last to leave or whatever, and if I am giving my all every game, then I deserve to be the man I want to be rather than the man other people want me to be.

"

Sonny Bill Williams, "Sonny Bill Williams regrets nothing", Brad Walter, *Sydney Morning Herald*, 29 November 2013

Jonah Lomu – arguably the most famous All Black worldwide – played from 1994 to 2002. He was 6 ft 5 inches tall and had a playing weight of up to 120 kg.

66

How do I tackle him? Wait until he's running past and bite his toes.

99

Former Irish winger Richard Wallace

CHAPTER
FIVE

CULTURE

There are fewer jokes in
New Zealand about yoghurt pots
and culture than there are across
in Australia.

Kiwis are notably proud of their
writers, artists, singers, bands and
film makers.

The 2018 Census showed 70% of New Zealand's population are Pākehā (New Zealand European), 16.5% are Māori, 15% Asian, 8% Pacific.

There are three official languages: Māori, English and Sign.

> **"**
>
> When we dream alone it is only a dream, but when many dream together it is the beginning of a new reality.
>
> **"**

Friedensreich Hundertwasser, Austrian artist and designer who lived in New Zealand from 1975 until his death on the *QE2* in 2000. His most famous building in NZ is the public toilets in Kawakawa, though an art centre was completed in 2022 in Whangarei.

Dame Kiri Te Kanawa

After starting out as a pop singer and entertainer, Te Kanawa won the Mobil Song Quest competition with the prize being a study trip to London, where she enrolled at the London Opera Centre. She had a stellar career, towards the end of which she perhaps closed yet another cultural circle after appearing as Dame Nellie Melba in an episode of *Downton Abbey*.

66

I grew up in the New Zealand countryside. We didn't have television until I was 14, so sing-alongs were our only entertainment.

99

Kiri Te Kanawa

The three highest-grossing New Zealand films

Hunt for the Wilder People (2016)

Boy (2010)

The World's Fastest Indian (2005)

The highest-grossing film made in New Zealand is *Avatar* (2009), followed by the *Lord of the Rings* and *Hobbit* films.

The ten most influential New Zealand songs

"Hoki Mai" – The Howard Morrison Quartet (Zodiac, 1959)

"Nature" – The Fourmyula (HMV, 1969)

"Tally Ho" – The Clean (Flying Nun, 1981)

"Poi E" – Patea Māori Club (Maui Records, 1984)

"Slice of Heaven" – Dave Dobbyn featuring Herbs (CBS, 1986)

"She Speeds" – Straitjacket Fits (Flying Nun, 1987)

"E Tu" – Upper Hutt Posse (Jayrem, 1988)

"How Bizarre" – OMC (Huh!, 1995)

"Sway" – Bic Runga (Columbia, 1997)

"Royals" – Lorde (Universal, 2013)

Grant Smithies, *Dominion Post*, 30 April 2022

The first ever single to be recorded in New Zealand was "Blue Smoke" in 1948.

The song was written by Ruru Karaitiana on a troop ship in World War Two and sung by Pixie Williams. Dean Martin later played a cover version.

D. H. Lawrence visited New Zealand in 1922 but stayed less than a day on his way from Sydney through to San Francisco. He apparently sent his erstwhile friend Katherine Mansfield a postcard from Wellington with only one word on it: "Ricordi", meaning "reminiscences" in Italian.

Virginia Woolf proclaimed that Mansfield produced "the only writing I have ever been jealous of". Their friendship and rivalry is also a subject of debate.

"

Make it a rule of life
never to regret and never
to look back. Regret is
an appalling waste
of energy, you can't build
on it: it's only good for
wallowing in.

"

Katherine Mansfield, born Wellington 1888, died France 1923

Actor Russell Crowe is another one that got away.

Born in Wellington, where he lived until he was four, he returned to Auckland for some of his secondary education.

Two of his cousins, Martin and Jeff Crowe, captained New Zealand Cricket.

The Lord of the Rings was so important for New Zealand that Pete Hodgson was appointed Minister of the Rings in the then government in 2001.

"

I first read *The Lord of the Rings* as an adolescent. It's a dense novel, a sprawling, complex monster of a book populated with a prolific number of characters caught up in a narrative structure that, frankly, does not lend itself to conventional storytelling. Imaginatively, this story is a filmmaker's dream, but translating it to the screen is quite another matter.

"

Peter Jackson, *New York Times*

"

It was amazing... We were dancing around like little dorks, but we looked around to our left and to our right and people were dancing like little dorks. The person on stage was dancing like a little dork. It was amazing to be in that environment, where the norm was to completely feel it.

"

Attendees at Lorde's 2022 concert in Seattle, reported in *Seattle Times*

"

With just a couple of acoustic guitars and a digital glockenspiel, they were maestros of every pop music style imaginable, although they concealed their talent with gags. 'You can tell when we've learned a new chord,' they told me, 'because we'll use it in our next three songs.' On stage, they played losers who thought they were winners. Off stage, they were winners who pretended to be losers.

"

Brian Logan in *The Guardian* on Flight of the Conchords

"

And we were like, lesbians? Lesbians? We must be lesbians! They're just like us! And you know what, from that day on afterwards, we identified as lesbians. There was no kind of angst or, 'Oh my god what's our parents going to do?', or do we have to fall in love first.

"

Lynda Topp of the Topp Twins, national treasures and comedy music duo, rnz.co.nz

66

I was told there was no place
for satire, New Zealanders didn't
really have a sense of humour,
and besides we had no right to
make fun of public figures. As the
project I was pitching required
all of those it did seem to be a
bit of a lost cause.

99

David McPhail, on pitching an idea to the New Zealand
Broadcasting Corporation in 1977 that was a forerunner to
McPhail and Gadsby, rnz.co.nz

"Ten Guitars" has been one of the best-loved songs at New Zealand backyard parties since the 1960s, and at one point every pop, rock and country singer in the nation had their own version. But the song was actually written for the king of romance, English crooner Engelbert Humperdinck.

Radio New Zealand, 2013, as seen on rnz.co.nz

❝

Money was not her god. She kept her work modest in size and in scale, and modestly priced because she wanted it to get into people's hands. And then she was, of course, very precious about whose hands it got into.

❞

Gallery owner Elva Bett, on New Zealand artist Rita Angus' attitude towards her paintings

"

We live at the
edge of the world, so
we live on the edge.
Kiwis will always
sacrifice money and
security for adventure
and challenge.

"

Lucy Lawless, imdb.com

66

People are like, 'Oh you just popped out of nowhere'. Yeah, but I worked for ten years straight before Marvel gave me a call. I was not just fucking around. I have evolved as a storyteller.

99

Taika Waititi, wired.co.uk

"

Yeah, I've got a few trolls who like to have a go at me. It doesn't bother me in any real way. Sorry for being so awful, or sorry for being lucky.

"

Dick Frizzell, arguably New Zealand's most famous living artist, is responsible for a lot of the country's more popular artwork, including The Four Square Man and 'Mickey to Tiki Tu Meke'

"

He sang. He danced. He drew. He joked. His live shows never failed to sell out and crowds flocked around him whenever he was out in public. He enjoyed popularity and wealth on a scale that had never been seen before in New Zealand.

"

Matt Elliott, *Billy T: The Life and Times of Billy T James*, 2009

"

I'm an introverted extrovert – I have enough confidence to do stand-up comedy, but I don't have the confidence to wear a hat.

"

Comedian Rose Matafeo

"

New Zealand ... is an egalitarian
nation made up of well over four
million rugged individualists and
naturally gifted sportspeople and
is run on alternate days by the
government and whoever bought
the national infrastructure.

"

John Clarke, aka Fred Dagg, 1948-2017, thestandard.org.nz

The 2018 Census showed 48% of the population had no religion, up from 29% in the 2001 Census.

In 2001, 53,000 people listed themselves as Jedi, but by 2018 this was down to 20,000.

The Booker Prize

Two New Zealand authors
have won the Booker:

Keri Hulme with
The Bone People in 1985

Eleanor Catton with
The Luminaries in 2013

Both David Bowie and ZZ Top vie for the biggest crowd ever in New Zealand, at the Western Springs Venue, with more than 80,000 attendees reported.

Hairy Maclary, with his friends Hercules Morse, Bottomley Potts, Muffin McLay, Bitzer Maloney and Schnitzel von Krumm, became absolute worldwide stars along with arch-enemy Scarface Claw – thanks to author and illustrator Lynley Dodd.

Five million copies of the series have been sold worldwide.

CHAPTER
SIX

KIWIANA

To many New Zealanders,
Kiwiana is simply all those weird
and wonderful, quirky things
from years gone by that have
contributed to a sense of identity
and nationhood, and help
to define what it is to be a Kiwi.

66

'Kiwiana' is just a quick way of saying 'things Pākehā feel nostalgic about'.

99

Seeking Sarah Tonin – Twitter

Try as you might to not include the "Buzzy Bee" toy, it is always top of anyone's list of Kiwiana.

This brightly coloured, traditional wooden toy has been a favourite with children for 75 years, and is the undisputed number-one Kiwi icon.

Number 8 wire

Another one on the "always-included" list. New Zealanders are supposed to have a "number 8 wire mentality", where they can fix everything or make anything with the standard-gauge wire.

The new way of fixing everything appears to be Duct Tape.

66

Don't die like an octopus; die like a hammerhead shark.

99

Māori proverb

Kiwis love...

gumboots, ponga shoots,
floppy hats, kiwifruits, beetroot,
Buzzy Bees, moggy cats, cabbage
trees, onions, kākāpōs, kia oras,
cheerios, Jandals, sandals, ketchup,
Coromandel's, Swanndris,
butterflies, mustard, fishing flies,
Hokey Pokey, Māori haka.

Kiwiburger, that's our tucker!

Excerpt from McDonald's ad, 1997

Kiwis love...

Sushi, cuppa-tea, lucky cats,
harmony, hot kai, league tries,
ketchup on a mince pie,
rainbows, chur bro, B-ball,
whanau, kilikiti, kapa haka.

Kiwiburger, that's our tucker.

Excerpt from updated McDonald's ad, 2020

The New Zealand accent was voted the sexiest in the world in 2019 by Big 7 Travel readers. Not everyone agrees.

"Fush and Chups", anyone?

The full Ka Mate Haka

Ka mate! Ka mate! (It is death! It is death!)

Ka ora! Ka ore! (It is life! It is life!)

Tenei te tangata puhuru huru
(This is the hairy person)

Nana i tiki mai
(Who caused the sun to shine)

Whakawhiti te ra
(Keep abreast! Keep abreast!)

A hupane kaupane! (The rank! Hold fast!)

A upane kaupane whiti te ra!
(Into the sun that shines!)

"God Save the Queen" is still listed as one of two official national anthems.

The other is "God Defend New Zealand", written by an Irishman, Thomas Bracken, and was adopted in 1977. Since the 1990s the first verse is sung in Māori, the second in English.

66

In some ways I believe
I epitomize the average
New Zealander: I have
modest abilities, I combine
these with a good deal
of determination, and I
rather like to succeed.

99

Sir Edmund Hillary

"

All science is either physics or stamp collecting.

"

Ernest Rutherford, born 1871 near Nelson, Nobel Prize winner and known as the father of nuclear physics

Koru

The Koru is a well-used symbol whose origin is the unfurling fern frond specifically from the ponga tree fern. It is commonly used within Māori art but has been appropriated by business.

Air New Zealand has a koru motif on its planes and many a New Zealand business person can be seen scurrying belatedly out of the airline's Koru Club having enjoyed the "free" hospitality before catching their commuter flight home.

Kiwi Shoe Polish

Invented in Australia in 1906
and sold around the world
in 180 countries, including New
Zealand. The inventor's wife was
a Kiwi – that's as close as it gets.

Jandals

Supposedly a word salad of Japanese Sandals. Jandals to the Kiwis are flip flops to the English and thongs to the Aussies.

Good Kiwis allegedly have two pairs; one for everyday use, one for best.

Bungy

New Zealand didn't really invent bungy jumping, but the first jumpers weren't too far away in Vanuatu.

The Oxford University Dangerous Sports Club made what can be considered the first modern bungy jumps, but it was New Zealand's A. J. Hackett who took it all on a phase and made the "sport" their own.

Queenstown was the site of the first commercial operation and has been going since 1988. New Zealand is regarded as the birthplace of this now global industry.

> **"**
> Oh oh no. Oh no.
> I'm beached, bro.
> I'm beached as.
> **"**

Blue Whale, written by Antony McFarlane and
Nick Boshier for the ABC in Australia, taking the piss
out of the New Zealand accent

"

Sex just can't be that good.

"

Green MP Denise Roche's response to controversial church leader Bishop Brian Tamaki blaming recent destructive earthquakes on homosexuality and "the weight of human sin"

In February 2016 then minister Steven Joyce had a dildo thrown at him by a protester while being interviewed on TV. As reported later...

"

The Economic Development Minister took it on the chin, as it were, joking later that it was simply one of the privileges of serving as an MP.

"

stuff.co.nz

"

If you distilled everything that was good in a New Zealand male at that time, Charlie would've been the Champagne or brandy you would've produced... He just seemed to sum up that Kiwi doggedness, resolve and self-effacement.

"

Author Tom Scott on Captain Charles Upham,
Victoria Cross with Bar, odt.co.nz

❝

However, I was most struck by their resilience. Every single one of them is a hero to me. We are a resilient nation anyway, but these are ordinary people going through extraordinary times with humour, grace, courage and empathy. I'm proud of them. I'm proud of us. This is us.

❞

Corinne Ambler, foreword of
This Is Us: Kiwis Abroad During Covid

As long as you're on public transport you can always tell a New Zealander anywhere in the world: when they get off the bus, they always thank the driver.